Clara Schumann

Janet Nichols Lynch

Pianist
and
Composer

*Clara
Schumann*

A Dragonfeather Book
Bedazzled Ink Publishing Company * Fairfield, California

978-1-949290-49-3 paperback

Cover Design
by

Sappling
Studio

Dragonfeather Books
a division of
Bedazzled Ink Publishing Company
Fairfield, California
http://www.bedazzledink.com

For Eva and Amelia

Table of Contents

Chapter 1
Bright Light

One spring day in 1824, four-year-old Clara Wieck sat in the nursery with her three younger brothers, Alwin, Gustav, and baby Victor. Clara was thin and petite with sloping shoulders. She had a pointed chin and wide, dark eyes. She was a serious girl who rarely smiled. Alwin and Gustav babbled in baby-talk, Victor wailed, but Clara was perfectly silent. Clara was always quiet—mute. She had not yet spoken a word. The people of Leipzig whispered gossip about her. Nearly five years old and not a single word out of her! The child must be simple. Maybe she was deaf. How tragic for Music Master Wieck to have such a daughter!

But Clara was not deaf. From her window seat in the nursery she could hear the customers downstairs, bustling in and out of her father's piano store to buy or rent sheet music. "Ping-ping" went the keys of the pianos as her father tuned them. The silvery tones of her mother's singing voice soared up the staircase. The piano music of her father's students rang out. Clara heard the glorious strains of music wafting through the house all day long.

Leipzig, a city in Saxony-Germany, was famous for its musicians and music publishing industry. The illustrious Johann Sebastian Bach had conducted the choir, played the organ, and composed in St. Thomas Church during the previous century. Later, the composer Felix Mendelssohn conducted the Leipzig Gewandhaus Orchestra and his sister Fanny, who also composed, opened her home to famous musicians from all over Europe. Busy highways and three converging rivers made Leipzig an important trade center. The wealthy merchants and craftsmen of the city were eager to spend time and money attending concerts and playing music in their own homes.

In Leipzig, a family of musicians was highly respected and could make a good living. Clara's father, Friedrich Wieck, loved music since he was a small boy, but his family was too poor to afford music lessons for him. Growing up, he was often cold, hungry, and sick. As an ambitious young man, he was determined to make a better life for himself. He studied at the University of Wittenberg, then worked as a tutor for children of rich families. He taught himself how to play and repair pianos. After tutoring for nine years, he borrowed money from a friend to open a store to sell pianos and give lessons. Through natural talent and hard work, Friedrich built the reputation of one of the finest piano teachers in Leipzig.

Clara's mother, Marianne Tromlitz Wieck, was a professional singer and often sang with the Gewandhaus Orchestra. Her first child, a daughter named Adelheid, was born in 1818, but died as a baby. Clara Josephine Wieck was born in Leipzig on September 13, 1819. Three boys were born in quick succession: Alwin in 1821, Gustav in 1823, and Victor in 1824. Clara's father chose her name, which means "bright light." He was determined to make her a famous pianist who would earn him the great fortune he coveted.

But how could Clara become a great musician if she couldn't even talk? Friedrich grew impatient waiting for her words. That spring day in 1824 he summoned his four-year-old daughter from the nursery, and when she arrived at his studio door, he lifted her onto the piano bench. He plucked out a short, easy tune from the keys.

"Now, Clara, play it just as I have."

Eager to please her father, Clara repeated the melody precisely as he had played it.

Friedrich tilted his head, his eyebrows raised. He played another piece, this time a little longer and more complicated. Clara raced her tiny hands across the keys, imitating the grace and style of her father's playing.

This time Friedrich smiled. Indeed, his Clara could not only hear, but she possessed great talent. With her hard work and his fine teaching, he would have a great pianist.

Chapter 2
A Star is Born

Clara's ears were quick to pick up music. Why, then, was she so slow to talk? No one knows for sure. It might have been because her parents were unhappy together and argued much of the time. Clara heard them hurl harsh, angry words at one another. Perhaps sensitive Clara shut out the cruel words and didn't try to repeat or understand them. Other times, the Wieck home was tense with Friedrich and Marianne's long, stony silences. Friedrich once remarked that Clara's nursemaid, Joanna, was "not talkative." Clara didn't hear many words from her daily adult companion so maybe that was why she didn't speak.

Marianne sang and practiced the piano for many hours a day. She also taught voice and Friedrich's advanced piano students. Friedrich was a better businessman and teacher, but she was a better pianist. Marianne waited on customers in the piano store and ran the Wieck household. She gave birth to five children in seven years. Yet it seemed she could never please her husband. She had been only nineteen when she married him, and he was twelve years older. Friedrich demanded that Marianne obey him, overloading her with work. He was often gruff, hot-tempered, and critical, but he rarely offered his wife praise and affection.

Marianne couldn't stand it any longer. In May, a couple months after Clara's first piano lesson, she fled to her parents' house in Plauen, ninety miles away, taking three-month-old Victor and Clara with her. Marianne knew that leaving Friedrich meant giving up her children. According to Saxony law, children were their father's property. This broke her heart, but she was too unhappy with Friedrich to live with him any longer.

Friedrich allowed Clara to spend the summer with her mother and grandparents in Plauen, but in September, four days after Clara's fifth birthday, Marianne tearfully returned her beloved daughter to her father's home. Friedrich let Marianne have custody of baby Victor, but he died at age two. At the time, very few couples got divorced, and the Wiecks were the subject of scandal in Leipzig. To add to the gossip, Marianne soon married Adolph Bargiel, another piano teacher and friend of Friedrich's. Adolph was kind and loving, and Marianne was happy in her second marriage. She had four more children with Adolph. Soon after they married, Adolph took over a music school in Berlin and moved his family there, over a hundred miles from Leipzig. Traveling between the cities was long and difficult. Clara called Marianne her "Berlin mother" and rarely saw her.

Clara ached for her mother. Her nursemaid, Joanna, who had been her caregiver since she was a baby, consoled her. Friedrich didn't like to see Clara clinging to Johanna. He fired the woman, claiming that she spoiled Clara. Clara felt lonely and abandoned in her father's house.

At age five, Clara began to speak. She never talked baby talk, but spoke in complete sentences. Even then, she didn't always respond when people talked to her. She was too busy thinking her own thoughts and listening to the music whirling inside her head. She didn't fully comprehend what people said to her until she was eight.

At age five, Clara began formal piano lessons with her father. In her first year of study, he didn't teach her to read music, but showed her how to copy the notes. He taught her to play all her pieces by ear. He wanted her to listen to music, not look at it on paper. He instructed her to pay close attention to the sound she produced on the piano. Her tone must "sing," he said. It must tug at the heart like the human voice. Clara was able to extract from the keys a rich tone quality like no other pianist. All her life she was praised for its warmth and feeling.

Friedrich had bold ideas about education that were new at the time. He didn't believe that children should "have to sweat for nine hours on hard school benches and pay for this with the loss of health and a happy childhood." He thought teachers should give students much individual attention. He said that outdoor exercise kept the mind sharp and the body strong.

By age seven, Clara followed a disciplined routine. Friedrich required all family members over the age of three to begin each day with a long walk, lasting several hours. He didn't slow down for the little ones, but expected them to keep up with the adults. Luckily, Clara could. She loved her walks and continued them throughout her life. She believed her daily walks brought her good health and a long life.

For two or three hours a day, a tutor taught Clara lessons in reading and writing in her own language, German. She also studied French and English, the two languages she would need when she toured Europe as a concert pianist. Other teachers provided her lessons in music theory, composition, and violin.

Clara took an hour piano lesson with her father every day, followed by two hours of practice. Friedrich encouraged Clara to make up little tunes on the piano. She composed her first pieces at age five, before she could read music. Clara loved to play the piano more than anything.

To punish Clara, Friedrich sometimes used her love of music against her. When he was unhappy with her piano playing, he refused to give her a lesson. Once he tore one of favorite pieces in half and ordered her to practice finger exercises the rest of the day. Alwin's punishment was crueler. When Friedrich didn't think the boy's violin playing was good enough, he grabbed him by the hair and threw him to the floor.

In the evenings, Friedrich took Clara to concerts, plays, and operas. He believed that she needed to hear all kinds of music to be a great musician herself. Clara's busy schedule left her no time to read for fun or play with other children.

When Clara was almost nine, her father remarried. His second wife was a young minister's daughter named Clementine Fechner. Clementine wasn't a musician. She was passive, willing to serve and obey Friedrich. She understood that his highest goal was making Clara a star, and she helped him any way she could. Clara still missed her own mother and probably wasn't very nice to Clementine. She never felt warm or close to her stepmother, no matter how hard Clementine tried to win her over.

The Wieck home was a gathering place for local and visiting musicians. These musicians performed new compositions from all over Europe that had never been heard in Leipzig. Clara played the piano for her father's guests. They were impressed with her talent and urged Friedrich to arrange a public concert for her. Friedrich, however, refused, telling them that his daughter wasn't ready. He didn't believe children should perform just because they looked cute. He wouldn't schedule any concerts for Clara until he felt she could play as well as an adult.

When Clara turned nine, Friedrich allowed her one brief public appearance. On October 20, 1828, Clara put on a while silk dress and took a carriage ride to the grand Gewandhaus concert hall. She walked on stage with her friend Emilie Reichold, another student of Friedrich's. The two girls performed a short piano duet.

The following day, a Leipzig newspaper reported, "It was especially pleasing to hear the young musically talented Clara Wieck, just nine years old. She has been trained under the direction of her experienced father, who . . . teaches with devotion and great skill."

Clara's concert career was officially launched!

Chapter 3
Robert

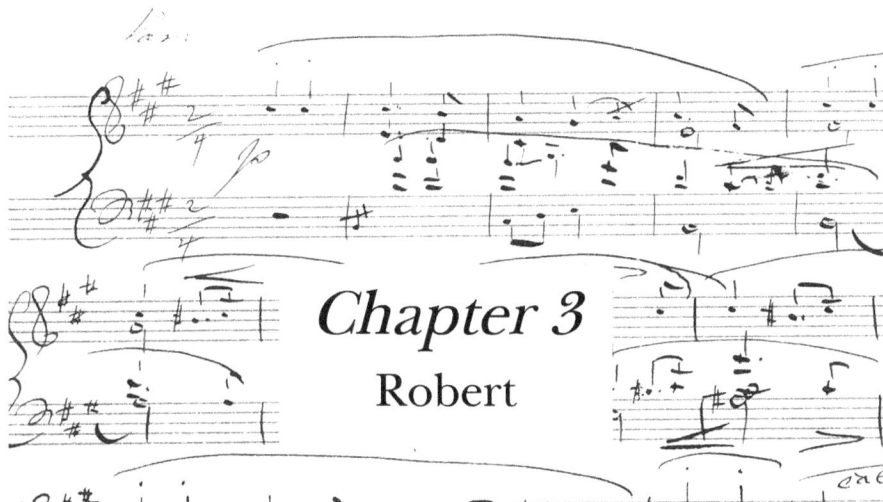

In the fall of 1830, Robert Schumann, one of Friedrich's students, came to live in the Wieck household. Robert acted like a big brother toward Clara, Alwin, and Gustav. He invited them to his room and told them bone-chilling ghost stories which Clara believed were true. He draped a white tablecloth over his head, his raised hands casting giant claw-like shadows over the candlelit walls, and chased eleven-year-old Clara around the room until she screamed with delight. He taught the children how to play charades. He conducted contests between the boys to see who could stand on one leg the longest. Robert was a twenty-year-old man, but he knew how to play more than the serious, disciplined Wieck children.

Robert Schumann was born in Zwickau, Germany, on June 8, 1810, the youngest of five children. His father, August, was a writer, publisher, and bookseller, who died when Robert was only sixteen. His mother, Johanna, was the daughter of a surgeon. Raised in a large, fun-loving family, Robert had been encouraged to use his vivid imagination in creative play. As the baby, he had been cuddled and pampered. He was horrified by Friedrich's violent temper and cruel treatment of his sons. He once wrote home to his mother, "Am I among humans?"

Robert and Clara played duets on the piano. They listened to each other practice and heard each other make up pieces. They shared their musical ideas so that they couldn't be sure who had thought up which tune first. Several times Robert and Clara used the same short melodies, called motives, in their individual compositions.

Before coming to live with the Wiecks, Robert had taken piano lessons with Friedrich for two years. His widowed mother had sent him to Leipzig to study law at the university, but he spent most of his time playing the piano and writing poetry. He begged his mother to let him drop out of law school so he could devote himself to music. Johanna worried that her son couldn't earn a living as a musician. Robert had played the piano since he was a child, but he had never been willing to practice much. Now Johanna feared her son was too old to try to become a concert pianist.

Johanna wrote to Friedrich asking his advice. Friedrich recognized Robert's musical talent, and he had great confidence in his own teaching. He also saw that he could make a fine profit from Johanna Schumann by hosting her son as a live-in student. Friedrich wrote back that if Robert was willing to do everything he told him, including all his finger exercises, he could make Robert "one of the greatest living pianists within three years."

While Robert lived in the Wieck household, Clara was practicing for her first public concert in which she would be the major performer. Clara's concert debut took place on November 8, 1930, at the Gewandhaus. She performed many pieces, including her own composition, *Theme and Variations*.

A Leipzig newspaper reported,

> This young artist's extraordinary accomplishment, in her playing as well as her composing, led to general astonishment and the greatest applause.

Robert was happy for Clara, but he was also jealous. This little girl had already made a smashing debut while he, a grown man, was sentenced to hours of boring finger exercises.

The following February, Hofmeister Music Company printed four of Clara's piano pieces, making her a published composer at age eleven. That same year, Robert also saw his *Abegg Variations* published as his first *opus*—Latin for "work."

When Clara was nearly twelve, Friedrich decided that she was ready to make her first long concert tour. He planned an eight-month journey, during which he and Clara would travel all the way to Paris, the musical capitol of Europe. Friedrich left behind Clementine, pregnant with their first child, Alwin and Gustav, his piano store, and all his students. This meant that Robert had to move out of the Weick's house. He was disappointed and angry, believing that Friedrich had treated him unfairly. Friedrich had promised to make him a famous concert pianist, the very career he was delivering to his own daughter instead.

Robert rented other rooms in Leipzig, while Clara and Friedrich embarked on their tour. For Clara, life on the road was exhausting. Her stingy father thought that the price of a hotel room was too big of an expense in any town where Clara wasn't giving a concert. Instead of resting in soft beds, Clara and her father traveled through the night in cold, bumpy carriages. For each of Clara's concerts, Friedrich made all the preparations.

He rented the hall, tuned and sometimes repaired the piano, advertised for the concert, and sold the tickets.

In addition to performing in public, Clara played concerts in *salons*, rooms in palaces or homes of wealthy music patrons. In return for her playing, Clara sometimes received gifts of rings, earrings, or gold chains. Friedrich preferred cash. He didn't let Clara keep any of her jewelry, but sold it to turn a profit for himself.

After months of traveling and performing, the Wiecks reached Paris. Compared to their little city of Leipzig, Paris was huge and overwhelming. Leipzig had three concert halls while Paris had over twenty. The famous composer-pianist Frederic Chopin and many other concert artists were already in Paris. They were stiff competition for an unknown twelve-year-old girl from Leipzig.

Friedrich Wieck did his best to impress the sophisticated and snobbish French. He wore yellow gloves and spoke French. He managed to introduce Clara to Chopin. He arranged for her to play in several salons. For each performance, he gave Clara a fashionable white silk gown to wear. The French were impressed with her playing, and soon her reputation grew. Finally, Friedrich felt Clara was well known enough in Parisian society to attract a large audience at a public concert.

Friedrich's timing was unfortunate. The serious illness cholera was sweeping through the city. Most people stayed in their homes or fled into the countryside to avoid the highly contagious disease. Only a few people attended Clara's concert. The Wiecks left Paris deeply disappointed. Clara hadn't made the big splashed Friedrich had hoped for.

Friedrich and Clara returned home, weary from their long journey. Clementine greeted them and joyfully presented to them her first child, four-month-old Marie. Alwin and Gustav were excited to have their sister Clara and father home again. They ran all the way to Robert Schumann's residence to report the news. The Wiecks threw a great homecoming party. At the celebration Clara performed Robert's new piano pieces, *Papillons,* which means "butterflies."

During the following weeks, Robert and Clara saw much of each other. They took long walks together and shared their thoughts. They exchanged musical ideas and called their compositions their musical "offspring." Clara was still only twelve, much too young to have a boyfriend, yet she was very mature. On tour she had seen much of Europe and had performed concerts like an adult. Robert and Clara behaved as good friends, yet they were growing closer day by day.

Robert continued to practice the piano, even though he was having physical problems with his right hand. Sometimes he couldn't move two of his fingers. This paralysis usually occurred just before he had to play a concert, and it might have been a form of stage fright. Robert caused further damage to his hand by using a device called a cigar mechanism. No one today is quite certain how it worked, but it was supposed to stretch the fingers faster than hours of practice. Robert injured his hand, and it never healed properly. His hope of a career as a concert pianist was dashed. At first, he was devastated, yet in time, he felt relief. He no longer had to compete with Clara and other virtuosos. He turned his back on performing and put all his energy into composing and writing.

In March 1834, Robert found a way to earn a living in music. With the help of four other musicians, including Friedrich Wieck, he became the editor and publisher of a weekly publication called *New Journal for Music.* Robert, who had inherited his writing talent from his father, wrote many articles, including reviews of performances and new compositions. Many music lovers at the time preferred the old Classical style of Haydn and Mozart; however, Robert encouraged his readers to hear the surprising new music of the Romantic era, including the work of Chopin, Mendelssohn, and Beethoven. His articles had a major influence on which composers would shape the music of the nineteenth century.

Meanwhile, Clara gave more concerts, mostly in nearby German towns and cities. She also continued to compose. Between 1833 and 1835, she wrote *Concerto for Piano, Op. 7*. A concerto is a long, important work for solo instrument and orchestra. Robert helped Clara with the orchestration, arranging her music so that all the instruments had parts to play. When Clara performed her concerto, people were amazed that a fourteen-year-old girl could compose such a huge, complicated piece. Most of them believed only men could compose music.

Friedrich appreciated Robert helping Clara with her composing, but he worried about how much time they spent together. Many young women married in their teens; however, Friedrich didn't want that for Clara. Marriage often meant the end of a woman's career, and he felt his daughter's star was only beginning to rise. He was suspicious of any men who saw her socially, and he controlled her every move. He told her what to write in her diary, and sometimes he wrote in it himself. He read all of her mail before she was allowed to see it. He always traveled with her and carefully guarded her.

In April 1934, Friedrich thought of a way to separate Clara and Robert. He sent Clara to Dresden to study singing and orchestration. His plan worked. In Clara's absence, Robert began courting seventeen-year-old Ernestine von Fricken, a friend of Clara's and a piano student of Friedrich's who boarded in the Wieck's house.

In July, Clara returned home for the christening of her new half-sister, Cacillie Wieck. The child's godparents were Robert and Ernestine, who acted very much in love. Robert had given Ernestine a ring, which made them informally engaged. He noted in his diary that Clara had returned from Dresden looking "very sad." It's a mystery if he understood why Clara was so upset.

Chapter 4
The Secret Engagement

One starry night in November 1835, two months after Clara's sixteenth birthday, Robert Schumann came to visit her. They had a wonderful evening of playing music and talking together. When it was time for Robert to leave, Clara lit the lantern and led him out to the front steps.

Robert took Clara into his arms and kissed her. He had kissed her many times before, but only like a brother. This kiss was different. Clara nearly dropped the lantern, feeling so dizzy she thought she would faint. She had been in love with Robert for years. She had often daydreamed of this very moment. At last, Robert saw her not as a childish playmate, but as a mature woman.

Clara took a step back, her head still reeling with joy and confusion. Fearfully, she glanced over her shoulder at the front window, where her father might be spying on her and Robert. Any moment he could dash out of the house to shame her and drive Robert away. But Clara didn't need to worry. Friedrich was no longer suspicious of Robert now that he was engaged to Ernestine von Fricken.

What about Ernestine? Clara wanted to know. Sheepishly, Robert stammered that their engagement had never been formal. He claimed he never loved her. He promised to break up with her the next time he saw her. Now, he only wanted Clara.

Clara was thrilled, but she worried what her father would do when he discovered that Robert was courting her. It took Friedrich several weeks to catch on, and when he did, he flew into a rage, throwing objects and stamping his feet. He forbade Robert to see Clara and whisked her off to Dresden to keep her apart from him. Desperately, she waited for her chance to meet with Robert. When she learned that her father would be out of Dresden for a few days, she sent a message to Robert asking him to meet her in secret. Robert arrived in Dresden, not joyfully, but grief-stricken. His mother had died. Clara consoled Robert as no one else could. In this shared state of mourning, they declared their love for one another.

When Friedrich found out about Robert's visit, he was so furious that he threatened to shoot him if he ever came near Clara again. He demanded that Clara return all of Robert's letters. As the dutiful daughter she was, Clara obeyed. She knew she was too young to go against her father's wishes. She had no hope of ever marrying Robert unless her father agreed to it. Under Saxony-Germany law, a man and woman, no matter how old they were, couldn't get married without their parents' permission.

For eighteen lonely, agonizing months, Clara and Robert honored Friedrich's wishes. All that time, the lovers didn't speak a word to each other nor write a single message. Friedrich didn't allow Clara to play Robert's music at public concerts. If they both happened to be attending the same concert or party, Robert kept his distance from Clara or quietly departed.

The separation of Clara and Robert caused a rift in the musical society of Leipzig. Musicians and their patrons were forced to take sides. Clara's friends gathered at her father's house, and Robert's friends gathered at another musician's house.

Worst of all, Robert and Clara had no idea what the other was thinking. Rumors drifted around Leipzig, causing Robert and Clara to doubt one another. Friedrich arranged for the singer Carl Banck to escort Clara in public so that he appeared as her suitor. Robert didn't review Clara's newly-published piano concerto in his *New Journal for Music,* but instead assigned it to another writer. This hurt Clara, who felt Robert had rejected her.

At last, Clara could no longer bear the silence between them. She insisted on playing his new composition *Symphonic Etudes* on an upcoming concert, and Friedrich gave her permission to do so. Clara then asked a friend to deliver the news to Robert. He wrote back, asking Clara to marry him. The following day, August 14, 1837, Clara sent her simple reply: "Yes." The couple was now secretly engaged, even though marriage still seemed impossible.

Robert asked Clara to deliver a formal proposal of marriage from him to her father on her eighteenth birthday. Robert was now the respected publisher, editor, and writer of the *New Journal for Music.* His compositions were played all over Europe. Certainly, Friedrich Wieck would now see him as a worthy husband for Clara. The fact that Friedrich allowed Clara to play his music in public made Robert think that Friedrich was ready to accept him as a son-in-law.

Clara, however, knew her strict father better than Robert did. She was afraid to give him Robert's marriage proposal. She needed courage and strength from Robert. After the year-and-a-half separation, she had to meet him, hug him, talk to him.

The couple managed to arrange a tryst; however, it was not as joyful as Clara imagined. She later wrote Robert, "You were so stiff, so cold." Robert and Clara had been apart so long that they didn't feel at ease with each other. Still, they decided to go ahead with their plans for marriage.

Clara handed her father Robert's marriage proposal and, just as she feared, he flatly refused it. Clara spent her eighteenth birthday in tears. Friedrich was not about to give Clara up to any man. He had made her a famous concert pianist. He believed that she was a success only because of his teaching and management. All the money she earned was legally his. Already, Clara had made him a rich man, but he was greedy for even greater wealth.

Robert wouldn't give up. He arranged an appointment with Friedrich to plead his case. Friedrich told him that Clara was too young to marry and that Robert couldn't earn enough to give her everything she needed. Robert left the Wieck house, defeated and humiliated.

Again, Friedrich forbade Robert and Clara to meet in private, however he did allow them to speak in public and write letters to each other.

Clara wrote to Robert, "Am I not a weak girl! I have promised my father to be happy for a few years yet, to live for art and for the world."

Clara wasn't weak, and she had her own ambitions. She wanted to continue her concert career as much as her father did. In the next month Clara and Friedrich left Leipzig and Robert behind, off to win over dazzling Vienna, Austria's illustrious musical center.

Chapter 5
Royal and Imperial Virtuosa

Clara was a smash hit in Vienna. The Viennese people jammed into the concert hall to hear her play. Each night her concerts were sold out. Fans who couldn't get tickets stormed the box office, and one night, a riot erupted. The police had to be called to restore order.

Most remarkable of all, the royal family awarded Clara with their highest honor, the title Royal and Imperial Virtuosa, naming Clara the greatest living concert artist. Amazing! Clara was very young and a woman! She wasn't even a citizen of the Austro-Hungarian Empire, and she wasn't Catholic, the religion of the royal family.

Clara created a new style of piano playing. She wasn't the strongest or the fastest pianist. Franz Liszt, another famous pianist and composer of the time, had made fast and loud playing popular, but it wasn't good enough for Clara. She didn't want to only entertain people; she wanted to move them. She made them feel love, sorrow, joy, and beauty. She chose only the finest music to play. She was the first pianist to play Beethoven's sonatas in a public concert after the great composer's death. Beethoven composed his last works when he was deaf. They are long, complicated, and difficult for the average listener to understand, but Clara knew how to draw out their beauty, and with her heartfelt interpretations, music lovers came to admire them. Of course, she included Robert's piano pieces on all her programs. The more people heard his music, the more famous he became.

Clara felt very deeply about the music she played. She wanted nothing to come between her and the music, not even the printed page. An actress doesn't hold a script when she performs, why should a pianist look at notes? Clara was the first pianist to play from memory in public. At first, this baffled the members of the audience. They found it distracting and thought it was a trick. Eventually, concertgoers got used to the idea. Other pianists began memorizing their music as well. To this day, concert pianists play from memory.

Clara performed in Vienna a long time, from October to May. Her success was even greater than Friedrich hoped it would be. Never did he imagine that his own Clara would become Royal and Imperial Virtuosa. Each concert, more and more money poured into his pockets. He wrote home to Clementine to rent a bigger house and buy rugs for the floor so that his little girls, Marie and Cacilie, wouldn't get cold feet.

Friedrich, however, didn't want to share the wealth with his sons, Alwin and Gustav. He wrote Clementine to find an old suitcase and send "these bad boys" out of the house to seek their own living. Only Friedrich, it seems, thought that his sons were bad. Clara and Robert could never understand why he was so unkind to them. Gustav, only fifteen, took an apprenticeship with a piano maker and became a musical instrument maker. Alwin went to work as a professional violinist, performing in several prestigious European orchestras. Friedrich also wrote a letter to

Robert, complaining that he wasn't writing enough about Clara in his *New Journal for Music.*

While in Vienna, Clara wrote to Robert, but only brief notes, late at night, standing at her hotel room dresser. If Friedrich caught her writing to Robert, he would insist on reading her letter. Robert addressed his letters to Clara with playful, imaginative names like "BCDE" and "Herr Kraus." Clara's friends claimed Robert's letters as their own at the Vienna post office, then put them in new envelopes addressed to Clara so that Friedrich wouldn't recognize Robert's handwriting on her mail.

Clara had a demanding schedule. After her evening concerts, she was expected to attend parties at the palace or in the homes of rich music patrons where she performed until midnight. She complained to Robert in a letter, "I have to play to people for a few pretty words and a cup of warm water . . . Is an artist much more than a beggar?"

Clara's letters to Robert were modest because she didn't want him to think she was becoming more important than him. She didn't want him to think she was having a good time without him. In truth, she loved to perform. She loved to be treated like a star. To her delight, a new cake was created in her honor: torte a la Wieck. The newspapers advertised it as a "light dessert that flies into the mouth of the eater." All her life Clara had worked for her career. She wanted to enjoy it, even if it meant being apart from Robert.

Chapter 6
Clara on Her Own in Paris

Clara returned home in May 1838. Both she and Robert were to spend the summer in Leipzig; however, he told her that he didn't want to try to meet secretly against her father's demands. He didn't want to sneak around stealing kisses from a girlfriend; he wanted a wife. He suggested that they set their wedding date for Easter 1840. They had been patient for the last two years. Robert said he could stand to wait for her two more years.

Clara, however, couldn't bear to be apart from Robert. She arranged meetings with him almost every day. To visit with him on his twenty-eighth birthday, Clara told him to come to her window at exactly nine in the morning. If he saw her wave a white cloth, that meant she would soon leave the house on an errand and meet him on the way. If he saw no signal, he should go away without hope of seeing her.

Friedrich suspected that Robert and Clara were meeting each other, but he had no proof. Once, after a friend of both Robert and Clara visited the Wieck's house, Friedrich had Clara's clothes searched for a message from Robert.

Although Clara was sometimes furious with her father's actions, she was sympathetic toward him. She loved both her father and Robert and felt torn between them. She wrote to Robert, "I am very upset when I see how miserable Father is when he thinks of losing me someday. I know my duty toward him and yet I love you endlessly."

Eventually, Friedrich discovered Clara and Robert were meeting. He ordered Clara to go on a concert tour to Paris without him. Clara was shocked! Robert thought Friedrich had lost his mind! At the time, a woman traveling without a male companion was unheard of. It was too dangerous. It wasn't proper. Robert wrote Clara, "You cannot travel alone. I won't permit it."

Robert, however, could do nothing to stop her. Friedrich was certain he had thought of the perfect way to teach his daughter a lesson. Not only did he expect Clara to fail without him; he wished for it. Clara would then see how much she still relied on him.

Friedrich hired a French woman, Claudine Dufourd, to be Clara's chaperone on the trip. On January 8, 1839, Clara and Claudine departed from Leipzig in heavy snowfall. Seated in the carriage each day, Clara wrote pages and pages to Robert. She complained of headaches, sleepless nights, and bothersome concert arrangements. Clara played several concerts on her way to Paris. She collected her own earnings for the first time.

In Stuttgart, Clara met Henriette Reichmann, a young woman her own age. Henriette wanted to take piano lessons from Clara, and she was willing to accompany her to Paris to do so. With her new friend, Clara didn't feel so afraid and alone. She dismissed her chaperone and traveled on with Henriette.

Finally, a month after she left Leipzig, Clara arrived in Paris. She felt anxious, remembering that she hadn't been a success there as a young girl of twelve. Robert's letters took weeks to reach her, and her father didn't write to her at all. She felt isolated, cut off from her loved ones. She found it difficult to make decisions about concert arrangements. She met with friends of her father who urged her to give up and go home. Clara was not easily discouraged.

Clara learned that a friend, Emilie List, was visiting Paris with her parents. The Lists invited Clara and Henriette to share their lodgings. Living with the Lists, Clara felt more at home in the big, foreign city. Clara and Henriette enjoyed operas, plays, and ballets. They went sightseeing at the royal palace, Notre Dame Cathedral, and the Panthéon. Clara practiced the piano, taught lessons, and planned her concerts.

At last, she realized that she could manage quite well on her own. She had watched her father conduct the business of her concerts for so long, that she had learned how to manage herself. She gave successful concerts at the Paris Conservatory, the Érard Salon, and elsewhere.

Favorable reviews in the newspapers and friends' reports of Clara's success reached Friedrich in Leipzig. His plan had backfired. Again, he resorted to threats. He wrote Clara that if she didn't give up Robert he would disown her and keep all her earnings. This time Friedrich had gone too far. Clara rebelled against him.

Chapter 7
The Fierce Court Battle

Robert and Clara were determined to marry whether Friedrich approved or not. Robert wrote a letter to him, asking one last time, for his permission to marry Clara. Clementine wrote back for her husband, "Wieck does not choose to have any connection with Schumann."

Robert then wrote a letter which he submitted to the Court of Leipzig, asking for legal permission to marry Clara without Friedrich's consent. He sent the letter to Clara in Paris. She signed it, then mailed it to the Court in Leipzig.

Robert sent money to Clara for her return trip from Paris, so that she could appear in court with him. When Clara arrived in Leipzig, Friedrich locked her out of the house. He didn't allow her to collect any of her clothes, personal things, or piano. Clara went to Berlin to live with her mother, Marianne, during the court proceedings. Although Clara had had little contact with her mother over the years, Marianne was happy to help her daughter any way she could.

Friedrich refused to give up Clara without a bitter fight. He was willing to do or say anything to prove that Robert would not be a worthy husband for her. He broke into her locked letter box and copied parts of Robert's personal letters in which he confessed any faults he had. Friedrich accused Robert of being a drunk who couldn't make a living. He called Robert "a mediocre composer whose music is unclear and almost impossible to perform." He even said Robert had bad handwriting and could barely speak! He argued that Clara wasn't fit to be a housewife because she had been raised as a concert pianist and knew nothing about housekeeping.

Friedrich sent letters to musicians throughout Europe, pleading with them to testify against Robert's character in court. Friedrich sent some of his letters to people in German cities where Clara was about to perform. He called her a "shameless girl" and warned fathers to keep their daughters away from her so they wouldn't be "poisoned" by her. He claimed that she was so immoral that she ruined any piano she played!

All this hurt Clara deeply, yet no matter how badly Friedrich behaved, she still loved him. Her father had started her piano lessons before she could talk. He had given her the self-confidence to succeed on the concert stages of Europe. He had managed all her business affairs and devoted his life to her career. He had offered her praise and love. Although she wasn't willing to give up Robert for him, she suffered a terrible loss in separating from him.

Finally, the dreaded day in court arrived. Friedrich was so upset, he erupted with angry outbursts, speaking out of turn. Several times, the judge had to silence him. Clara couldn't bear to see her father scolded and disgraced. Friedrich stood alone, with no one to support his cause. He hadn't found anyone who would testify against Robert. Most people liked him. Furthermore, musicians and composers weren't willing to speak out against such an important music critic. They knew Robert and Clara were devoted to each other and how much they had suffered because of Friedrich. The judge decided the case in their favor. On August 1, 1940, the court granted Robert Schumann and Clara Wieck permission to legally marry without parental consent.

Afterward, Friedrich turned his back on his beloved daughter, Clara, and began to train her half-sister, Marie, for the concert stage. He was so confident in his teaching and managing that he believed he could make any girl into a superstar pianist. Marie did become a fine pianist, but she lacked great talent and was never as successful as Clara. She never married, but remained loyal and obedient to Friedrich until his death.

Friedrich kept all the money Clara had ever earned. Clara had made a fortune, but now she was penniless. She spent the week before her wedding playing concerts, trying to earn a little money for her wedding clothes and linens. Robert had supported her and her widowed mother for the past year, and he had bought her a piano to practice on. She felt ashamed that she had no dowry, "like any simple middle-class girl." Robert assured her that he didn't care about the money. He possessed the greatest prize of all. He had won Clara to be his wife.

Chapter 8
Robert's Wife

Clara and Robert were married on September 12, 1840, one day before her twenty-first birthday. The small wedding took place in a village church outside of Leipzig. During the ceremony, Clara bowed her head and prayed "that God may keep Robert in good health for many, many years."

As a newlywed, Clara was happier than she had ever been. She took time off from playing concerts to stay home with Robert. For so long they had been forced apart, seeing each other for short, stolen moments. Now, at last, Clara and Robert could be together day and night. They took long walks, arm in arm. They played music together. They started a marriage diary. Frist, Robert wrote in the diary for one week, then Clara wrote in it for a week, taking turns for many years.

Eighteen-forty is called Robert's "song year." His love for Clara inspired him to compose many beautiful songs. Clara wrote songs, too. Robert put some of his songs with some of hers. He named the collection *The Springtime of Love* and sent it to his publisher. At the time, people thought that only men could compose great music. Only a few women dared to publish their compositions. Women composers were afraid that critics would embarrass them with bad reviews. Their family names would be put to shame. They would be called "unladylike" for trying to do a man's work. Their music would be put down as mere "women's work."

Robert didn't agree with this. He thought Clara was a fine composer, and he was proud of her creative work. Robert played a joke on the critics who were so certain that a woman's compositions were inferior to a man's. He simply wrote "by Robert and Clara Schumann" on the title page of *Springtime of Love*, not revealing which songs he had composed and which were Clara's. The critics couldn't figure it out. They didn't dare try because they didn't want to embarrass themselves by guessing wrong.

After a few months of newlywed happiness, Robert began to compose again for many hours a day, leaving Clara alone much of the time. He closed himself up in his room, shutting Clara out. He rarely shared his music with her while he was working on it. To make things worse, Clara couldn't work on her own music. Robert needed complete silence when he composed, and their house was small. Clara was used to practicing the piano five or six hours a day, and now she couldn't play at all. She had labored all her life for music, and now she had to sit idle for most of the day. She wept and hid her tears from Robert.

She wrote in her diary: "My piano playing is falling behind. This always happens when Robert is composing. There is not even one little hour in the whole day for myself! If only I don't fall too far behind . . . I can't do anything with my composing. I would sometimes like to strike my dumb head!"

Clara knew Robert was a great composer long before the rest of the world realized it. One of the reasons she had fallen in love with him was because of his beautiful music. She believed in him and wanted to be supportive. That meant her piano playing would have to be sacrificed for his composing, even though Clara was one of the greatest pianists in the world.

During the nineteenth century, a married woman was expected to stay at home and care for her family and household. Robert assumed that after they married, Clara would be content playing the piano at home, for him and their musical friends. He didn't realize that this was not enough for Clara. She longed for the crowded auditorium filled with people clapping and shouting her name. She craved the bright stage lights and full orchestra accompanying her. Every time Clara thought about performing, her fingers tingled and her heart beat faster.

Clara's chance to return to the stage came six months after her wedding. She was invited to perform in a benefit concert to raise money for the Gewandhaus orchestra musicians' retirement fund. The Schumanns' good friend Felix Mendelssohn would be conducting, and Robert's First "Spring" Symphony would be premiered on the program. Clara eagerly accepted the offer to take part in the gala concert.

Clara's stage name was Clara Wieck, but she boldly changed it. On March 31, 1841, she performed a concert as Clara Schumann for the first time. This made Robert proud and happy. He thought it was a meaningful way for Clara to show her love and devotion to him.

Backstage, waiting for her turn to play, Clara shook with fright. Perhaps some of her fans in the audience wouldn't recognize her with her new name. She worried that she was making a terrible mistake trying to perform again. She was no longer used to playing for a large crowd, and she hadn't been able to practice much.

When Clara walked on stage the applause was thunderous. It continued, even as she sat at the piano, waiting to begin. Never before had she heard such an enthusiastic reception for any concert artist. She claimed later that she turned "pale and red." Robert wrote in their marriage diary, "My Clara played everything like a master and in such an inspired mood that everyone was enchanted."

Chapter 9
Motherhood

At the time of the Gewandhaus Benefit Gala, Clara was three months pregnant with the first of eight Schumann children. Nineteenth century women didn't appear in public once their pregnancies showed. Clara, however, continued to give concerts until one week before giving birth, just as her own mother, Marianne, had done.

On a stormy night, September 1, 1841, Marie Schumann came into the world amid thunder and lightning. Robert and Clara became new, proud parents. Clara told everyone her new little daughter looked exactly like Robert. Clara cooed and fussed over her baby. Whenever Marie cried, Clara played the piano for her until she fell asleep.

Clara worried about Marie's health. She feared she wasn't producing enough milk for Marie, and in her diary she called her baby "half-starved." When Marie was a month old, Clara hired a wet-nurse to feed her. Marie got enough to eat, and Clara got more freedom. She began plans for a concert tour lasting four months that would take her all the way to Copenhagen, Denmark.

The journey would be too difficult for baby Marie. Clara left her behind, in the care of her wet-nurse and Robert's brother Carl and his family. Robert didn't want to go on tour, but as Clara's husband, he felt it was his duty to escort her. Robert and Clara left Leipzig on January 1, 1842, traveling north toward Hamburg, Germany. From the beginning of the trip, Robert was unhappy. He worried that something terrible would happen to Marie while they were away. He fretted that the editor he had hired to take over his *New Journal for Music* wouldn't do a good job. He was so upset he couldn't compose. His health was poor most of the trip. In Oldenburg, a duchy in Northern Germany, the Duke and Duchess threw a grand reception for Clara, but didn't invite Robert. Clara went off to the party unescorted, rationalizing that Robert was a shy man who didn't like talking to strangers. She assumed he would be more comfortable alone in their hotel room. When she returned to the hotel, flushed and bubbling over with the excitement of the party, she was surprised to find Robert hurt and angry. He announced that he had had enough of her concert tour. He wanted to go home.

Clara pleaded with him. She didn't want to cancel her concerts in Copenhagen. The people of Denmark were expecting her to play for them, and they were eager to hear Robert's music. After much discussion, Robert decided to return to Leipzig while Clara traveled on alone to Copenhagen. This was a daring move. Clara would have to cross the treacherous Baltic Sea, a journey that took all night. She was afraid, having never embarked on such a long sea journey. To make matters worse, a storm raged over the cold, choppy water and twice the crossing had to be postponed. Clara suffered from self-doubt. Was the storm God's way of telling her not to go to Copenhagen? Would she be shipwrecked and drowned? Would this be her punishment for leaving behind her husband and baby daughter?

At last, the weather cleared up. Clara sailed across the water safely. In Copenhagen, her performances and Robert's compositions were a big success. Meanwhile, at home, Robert was worried sick about Clara and couldn't compose. He was furious with Friedrich who had spread the false rumor that Robert and Clara's marriage had already failed, and they had separated.

Clara decided that her concert tour had caused too much strain on her marriage. For the next two years, she played concerts close to home. She then got the urge to travel once more. She planned another four-month tour, this time to distant Russia. Again, Robert hated to go. There were now two tiny daughters to leave behind with Uncle Carl. Elise had been born April 25, 1843. Trying to look on the bright side, Robert finally agreed to accompany Clara. The Schumann family needed the money she would earn. It was a good opportunity to have his music played in Russia where it was not yet well-known. A break from the strain of publishing the New Journal for Music would do him good and give him more time to compose.

The Schumanns' journey over vast, empty Russia was brutal. Often Robert and Clara rose at three in the morning to be on their way by four. The desolate white landscape was bitter cold. Robert and Clara mostly traveled by sleigh over ice and snow, bundled up in piles of furs.

Traditionally, a single concert was performed by many musicians. Usually a full orchestra played, singers sang, and small groups of musicians played their instruments. The soloist or star of the concert appeared for a small portion of the program. In contrast, Clara gave many long concerts in Russia, unassisted by any other musicians. She was one of the first concert artists to perform entire recitals alone.

Clara was well-received all over Russia. She was named an honorary member of the St. Petersburg Philharmonic Society. She performed at the Winter Palace for Tsar Nicholas I and Tsarina Alexandra. She earned a great deal of money—6,000 thaler. Thalers were silver coins used in Germany and other European countries. In Russia, Clara had a wonderful time performing, sightseeing, and being entertained by music patrons. She loved being the center of attention and living the life of a glamorous star. She wasn't looking forward to returning to Leipzig, to keep house and care for babies.

Robert, however, was sick and depressed most of their time in Russia. He suffered from homesickness, fever, pain, and dizziness. During one illness, he thought he was going blind. A doctor told Robert he suffered from "nervous fever." Clara didn't seem to realize how serious his illness was.

Soon after Clara and Robert returned from Russia, Robert sold his *New Journal for Music.* He had published the journal for ten years. His work of writing and editing often left him too exhausted to compose. Giving up the journal, however, may not have been the best decision for his mental health. While composing, Robert listened only to his own thoughts. He worked night and day until he completed a piece. Each composing session left him weak, both in body and mind. The *New Journal from Music* gave him work to do between compositions and opportunities to interact with other people. Now, he had no connection with the outside world.

In August 1844, Clara began teaching piano at the Leipzig Conservatory, a famous music school where Robert also taught. They both resigned, however, when Robert suffered another physical breakdown. This time his illness was more serious than "nerves." Robert was too weak to walk across the room. For eight days he trembled and wept. At night, he couldn't sleep and had frightening vision of demons. Robert was fighting for his sanity. Mental illness ran in his family. His father had died insane and his older sister, Emilie, had gone mad and committed suicide by jumping out a window.

Robert recovered, but Clara was deeply concerned about his health. She thought a change of scene would do him good, and Robert agreed. The Schumanns decided to move to the charming little town of Dresden. In December 1844, the Schumann family packed their belongings and traveled to a new home.

Chapter 10
Escape from Dresden

Dresden, home of the Royal Court of Saxony, was very different from the industrial trade center of Leipzig. The broad Elbe Rover rolled lazily through Dresden and green, rounded hills surrounded the pretty town. The air was clear and the skies were blue. There were lush parks and gardens, stately homes and beautiful churches. The royal palace was a magnificent structure and the grand opera house offered wonderful productions. The Schumanns were certain Dresden would be a lovely place to live.

Throughout the winter and spring of 1845, Robert and Clara studied the music of Johann Sebastian Bach. Bach, who had lived a hundred years before them, wrote counterpoint, an old style of music in which many melodies intertwine. The challenge of writing counterpoint was creating interesting melodies that harmonized with one another. This was a god thinking exercise for Robert, and it seemed to help his mental health. Slowly, he regained his physical strength.

Using what she had learned from Bach's music, Clara composed in counterpoint a set of preludes and fugues for piano. She also composed one of her finest works, *Piano Trio in G Minor, Op. 17*, for violin, cello, and piano. Robert and Felix Mendelssohn thought Clara's trio was an exceptional work. It was played often during the nineteenth century, and musicians also play it today.

Robert composed some of his most important works including *Symphony in C Major* and *Piano Concerto in A Minor*, which Clara premiered in Dresden. Robert also wrote *Album for the Young,* a collection of short, easy piano pieces for his children to play. The most popular of these, often played by piano students today, are "The Merry Farmer" and "Soldier's March."

While living in Dresden, Clara spent most of her time and energy caring for Robert and the children and managing the household. She taught a few piano students to earn a little money. She gave birth to four children within five years. The Schumanns' third daughter, Julie, was born on March 11, 1845. Their long-awaited first son, Emil, was born February 6, but, sadly, he lived only sixteen months. The births of two other sons followed: Ludwig, named after Beethoven, on January 20, 1848, and Ferdinand, on July 16, 1849.

Clara performed in a few concerts, mostly in Dresden and Leipzig, a four-hour train ride away. All her other concerts were in German cities: Vienna, Berlin, Zwickau, and Hamburg. Clara longed to travel on a concert tour to far-off countries, but she rarely complained, even in her private diary. She felt Robert and their children needed her at home.

Life in Dresden was usually quiet. However, the Schumanns had one harrowing adventure. In May of 1849, rebels revolted again the Royal Court of Saxony. Previously, there had been uprisings in Vienna and Berlin. At the time, Germany was not a single country, but consisted of small regions called principalities, each with its own ruler and government. The rebels believed that the German people would be stronger under one federal government. They were trying to overthrow the royal families in order to unite Germany into one country.

Fighting broke out in the streets of Dresden. Bells clanged in all the church towers. Guns fired and cannon balls thundered. The pavement and sewers were torn up and used as barricades during the battle. The royal family called in troops from neighboring Prussia and paid them to put down the rebels. Many of the rebels were killed by these Prussian soldiers, called mercenaries, who were only fighting to earn money. The Prussians laid the dead out in the streets to warn other citizens not to fight.

The rebels were courageous fighters, unwilling to surrender. They drafted every able-bodied man in Dresden, pounding on doors and demanding that all male citizens fight on their side. When the rebels marched up to the Schumanns' residence, Clara told Robert to hide. The Schumanns believed in the rebels' cause of a unified Germany, but Robert wasn't willing to go to war for it. He was still ill, and even in good health he was not fit to be a soldier.

Clara told the rebels that Robert wasn't home. They departed, but she knew they would be back. To keep Robert safe, she would have to smuggle him out of Dresden. If she tried to flee with all the children, the rebels would notice them, seize Robert, and force him to join their army.

Clara, seven months pregnant with Ferdinand, decided to take only Marie with her and Robert. When the coast was clear, they sneaked out the back door, leaving behind Elise, Julie, and Ludwig, ages six, four, and one-and-a-half, in the care of servants. Clara, Robert, and Marie rode the train for eight miles to Mügeln, then walked to a nearby village. From that distance, they still could hear the cannons booming in Dresden.

One anxious day passed and then another. Clara worried constantly about the children that they had left behind. Still, it wasn't safe for Robert to return to Dresden. The next day, at three in the morning, Clara set off for the city, accompanied by two other women. The women took the train as far as they could, then trudged across open fields, with Clara holding the weight of her pregnancy in her arms. Along the way, they saw many Prussian soldiers. Clara didn't know if the soldiers would draw their swords on women or not.

When the women finally reached the Schumann house, they found the children safe and sound, asleep in their beds. Clara woke them up and packed a few clothes. Soon the women and children walked back across the fields to safety. Meanwhile, Robert shut himself up and composed, turning his back on the danger.

A month later, the Schumanns returned to Dresden to find much of the beautiful city in ruins. Cannon balls had poked gaping holes into houses and knocked down whole walls. The opera house had been burned to the ground. Many people had been killed.

The Schumanns didn't live in Dresden much longer. The audiences who attended their concerts didn't know much about music. They didn't understand Robert's work, so they didn't like it. Clara thought their family should move to a larger city where their musical talent would be more appreciated.

The city of Düsseldorf offered Robert the position of music director of the Düsseldorf Orchestra and Chorus. This sounded like a good opportunity, but Robert was reluctant to take the job. For one thing, it didn't pay much. It involved a tremendous amount of work, rehearsing and performing ten full concerts and four church services a year. Robert didn't have much experience conducting, and he didn't enjoy it. He wanted to spend his time composing. After much consideration and against his better judgment, he accepted the post. The Schumanns packed up once again and moved to Düsseldorf in September 1850.

Chapter 11
Trouble in Düsseldorf

In Düsseldorf, Clara was busier than ever. The Schumanns rented a house large enough for her to use her piano at the same time Robert composed. She taught piano lessons and practiced so that she could perform in many of Robert's concerts. She composed *Variations on a Theme of Robert Schumann for Piano*, *Three Romances for Piano*, *Three Romances for Violin and Piano*, and *Six Songs*. On December 1, 1851, she gave birth to Eugenie, the Schumanns' seventh child and youngest daughter.

The people of Düsseldorf were avid fans of Clara's piano playing, and they were proud to have the renown composer Robert Schumann employed by their city. Despite this, Robert had problems with his job from the start. He had little talent for conducting. He didn't have the right personality to take command of so many musicians in a full orchestra and chorus. In rehearsals, he didn't tell the musicians much about how he wanted the music to sound. He spoke so softly that most the musicians couldn't hear him. He dropped his baton so often that he tied it to his wrist with a string, which made him look silly. Many of the musicians lost respect for him and were noisy and disruptive at the rehearsals. Some of them stopped attending.

As a result, the performances of the Düsseldorf Orchestra and Chorus weren't polished. The audience members didn't enjoy the concerts. Some people complained to city officials that Robert wasn't doing a good job.

Clara knew Robert was struggling, but she wouldn't admit it to anybody, not even herself. Instead, she tried to help him. She started attending rehearsals to tell the musicians what Robert wanted them to do. She sat at the piano to help the chorus members learn their singing parts. The musicians were amazed that a star concert pianist would take the lowly position of a rehearsal accompanist.

Robert appreciated Clara's help, but he also resented it. It bothered him to see how capable Clara was of taking charge of the rehearsals and getting things done, when he was failing at it. He began to lash out at her. He told his assistant director to play the piano for the chorus rehearsals, explaining that, "The piano drumming tired Clara and was more suitable for a man." While Clara was practicing for a performance of Robert's *Quintet in E-flat Major,* he replaced her with another pianist, saying, "A man understands that better." After one of Clara's magnificent performances, Robert told her that her playing was "terrible," while she thought she had played as well as ever. Never before had Robert mistreated her. She thought if he could dismiss her so rudely and say such awful things to her then he must not love her anymore. She was crushed. She hid in her room and wept bitterly.

For a long time, Clara had yearned to perform in England. She began to make plans for a concert tour there only to discover that she was pregnant again and would have to postpone the trip.

In her diary, she wrote, "My last good years are passing, my strength too . . . I am more discouraged than I can possibly say."

Robert and Clara were deeply troubled. It seemed that all the happiness had faded from their marriage. One day, a stranger came to visit them, delivering renewed joy, just when they needed it most.

Chapter 12
The Young Blond Stranger

It was almost noon when the Schumanns' doorbell rang. Twelve-year-old Marie ran outside to find a handsome young man with bright blue eyes and long blond hair curling over his shoulders. The stranger asked to see Robert Schumann.

"My parents went out," Marie said.

The stranger asked when he could come again.

"Tomorrow at eleven," Marie replied.

The stranger was Johannes Brahms, a young composer only twenty years old, who lived in Hamburg. Not very many people had heard Brahms' compositions, which had not yet been published. Brahms was also a fine pianist who had given his first solo concert at age fifteen. He was a friend of the famous violinist Joseph Joachim, who was also a friend of the Schumanns. Joachim thought Robert would be willing to help Brahms with his composing career. Brahms, who was shy and modest, didn't think Robert would want to be bothered with a young, unknown composer. Introducing himself to the Schumanns took a lot of courage.

The following day, Brahms returned to the Schumanns' house with his knapsack filled with the compositions he had written in the previous three years. Robert invited him in and asked him to play his music on the piano. Brahms had played only a few measures, when Robert jumped up, exclaiming excitedly, "Please wait a moment. I must call my wife." Robert knew Clara would want to hear Brahms' music, too.

Robert ran and got her. As Brahms played his piano pieces, Robert and Clara listened intently. The Schumanns didn't always like the same music, but they agreed that Brahms' compositions were brilliant. It had been a long time since they had heard such startling, new harmonies. They were certain that they had discovered a great composer.

Robert and Clara gave Brahms so many compliments that the timid, young man became embarrassed. He could hardly believe that two such important musicians were so enthusiastic about his music, and yet, deep down, he *knew* his music was something special.

When it was time for Brahms to leave, the Schumanns invited him to return the next day. As Robert and Clara sat down to have lunch with their children, they were excited about Brahms' music. Again and again, either Robert or Clara interrupted the conversation to say something about Brahms. They could hardly speak about anything else.

Brahms visited Robert and Clara almost every day for a month. The Schumanns enjoyed the person as much as they appreciated his music. Together, the Schumanns and Brahms talked, took long walks, and read. They played and listened to music for hours at a time. Robert and Clara were delighted to have Brahms with them. He probably reminded them of the sweet, early days of their marriage, when they were young and healthy, with few cares in the world except each other and music.

Brahms left Düsseldorf for Leipzig on November 2. In his knapsack, he carried a letter of recommendation from Robert to Robert's music publisher, Breitkopf & Hartel, urging them to publish Brahms' music. The publisher took Robert's advice and Brahms' first works appeared in print. Robert hadn't written anything about music for ten years, but he thought Brahms' fresh, bold style was important enough to break his silence. He wrote an essay called "New Paths" which was published in *New Journal for Music.*

Soon after Brahms left Düsseldorf, the Schumanns received devastating news. Two members of the Düsseldorf Music Society visited the Schumanns to report that Robert was dismissed from his duties as music director.

This shouldn't have been such a terrible blow. Robert should have been relieved that he didn't have to continue a job he disliked. His talent was in composing, and that is what he preferred to do. Still, Robert's pride was wounded. He couldn't admit that he wasn't suited for conducting. Clara couldn't either. She blamed the orchestra and chorus members for the poor performances. Both the Schumanns felt insulted and disgraced.

Robert and Clara tried to leave their troubles behind by going on a month-long concert tour in Holland. Robert conducted many of the concerts in which Clara performed. The Dutch audiences received Robert and Clara warmly. The Schumanns dined on rich Dutch food and good drink. They returned home to spend Christmas with their children. In January, they traveled to Hannover and enjoyed a visit with Joachim and Brahms. They tried to carry on their lives, enjoy themselves, and forget that Robert had been fired.

Robert couldn't let it go. He grew more and more depressed. By February, he couldn't sleep, and he suffered painful headaches. Music played continuously in his mind. Whenever this happened before, he turned to composing, but this time he couldn't organize the sounds into a composition. This time, the music inside his head tormented him. Sometimes a single note droned on and on, and other times a whole orchestra played music which sounded to him like singing angels. Then the angels turned to devils, whizzing over his head. Robert screamed in terror.

Clara sent for doctors who managed to calm Robert down. Still Clara was deeply concerned. She wrote in her diary, "Where will it all end?"

Chapter 13
Clara's Greatest Sorrow

On Sunday evening, February 26, 1854, Robert abruptly rose from the sofa and announced to Clara that he had to go to the insane asylum because he could no longer control his mind. He said he feared his own actions, that he might even try to harm Clara or the children.

Clara, five months pregnant with their eighth child, couldn't believe Robert was really losing his sanity. He had suffered nervous breakdowns before. Certainly, all he needed was rest and quiet. She sent for the doctor. Robert began to collect things to pack: watch, money, music, paper, pens, and cigars. He asked Clara for his clothes.

"Robert," she pleaded, "is it your wish to abandon your wife and children?"

"Yes," he replied. "It won't be for long. I'll come back recovered."

The doctor examined Robert and sent for a male nurse to spend the night with him. The nurse soothed Robert. Robert talked politely with him, read the newspaper, and fell asleep. Clara stood outside his door, listening, thinking he might call for her. She was used to sitting up with Robert on the nights that he couldn't sleep. She wanted to comfort him now. Robert didn't ask for her. At last, she accepted the separation from him and went to bed herself.

The next morning Robert got up, but he was the saddest Clara had ever seen him. She walked up to him and hugged him.

"Oh, Clara," he exclaimed. "I'm not worthy of your love."

She told him it wasn't true. "I've always looked up to you with the greatest, deepest respect," she replied.

Later that morning, more doctors came to talk to Clara about Robert's mental health. Clara asked Marie to sit in her room and watch the hall, in case Robert came out of his room and asked for anything.

Suddenly, Robert appeared in the hall, wearing a green-flowered robe. He gave Marie a horrified looked, then held his hands before his face and muttered, "Oh, God."

Marie was shocked by her father's appearance. She had never seen him look so upset. She sat still, trying to think how she could help him. In the next moment, she realized that he was gone. Marie assumed that he had returned to his room. When she looked for him there, she discovered he had vanished. Marie screamed and ran to find her mother. Everyone searched the house for Robert.

Meanwhile, Robert had slipped down the hall, into the yard, and out the front gate. Still dressed in his night shirt and robe, he shuffled down the street, sobbing in the pouring rain. He reached the toll bridge over the Rhine River and dug into his pocket for some coins. Finding none, he offered his red silk handkerchief as payment for crossing the bridge. Then, before the attendant could stop him, he ran halfway across the bridge, flung his wedding ring into the swiftly moving water, then leaped in himself.

Some fishermen pulled Robert into their boat, saving him from drowning. Robert tried to jump out of the boat, but the fishermen held him down until they could get to shore. They walked Robert down the street, holding him up beneath his arms. People crowded around the famous composer, some of them dressed in bizarre costumes to celebrate the pre-Lenten season. Grimly, Robert trudged along, dripping wet, his face in his hands.

In this way, Clara saw Robert stumbling toward her. She broke down and sobbed. The doctors led her away. They told her a meeting with Robert now would only upset him more. The doctors worried about Clara's health, too. They thought the Schumanns needed to be apart. They urged Clara to go stay in the home of her blind friend, Rosalie Leser, and her companion, Elise Junge.

Robert was brought home and left under the care of two male nurses, who stayed with him day and night. Clara's mother, Marianne, arrived from Berlin to run the Schumann household and take care of the children.

The doctors didn't allow Clara to see Robert. Instead, she received reports about his health every hour. Robert didn't ask for Clara. He didn't seem to miss her. He was glad to have the male nurses for company. He spent the rest of the day at his desk copying out a new composition. For a few hours, it seemed like he might recover.

Then he grew violently upset. He begged his doctors and nurses to take him to the insane asylum. He was certain that he would get better if he were allowed to go there and rest. His nurses put him to bed and didn't allow him to get up again.

Five miserable days slowly passed. Clara waited at her friend's home, anxious to hear the news about Robert. She sent him a gift of oranges and violets. Again, she asked to see him, but the doctors forbid it. They suggested that Robert be sent to a small, private asylum in Endenich, near Bonn. Clara was against the plan. She still thought Robert could recover at home. At last, the doctors convinced her to send Robert away.

The next day, Saturday, March 4, a carriage bound for Endenich arrived at the Schumann home. The driver turned into the courtyard out of the neighbors' sight. From an upstairs window, the Schumann children watched their father get into the carriage. That was the last they saw of him.

Clara was still staying at Rosalie Leser's home. She didn't get to say good-bye to Robert nor watch the carriage depart. Robert didn't ask to see Clara nor his children. Clara sent a bouquet of violets to him. On the journey to Endenich, he handed the violets to the other passengers.

Grief-stricken, Clara returned home. Her beloved Robert was gone. She didn't know when he would be back, if ever. It was hard for Clara to imagine life without him. When she was a girl, he had been like a big brother to her. When she was an overworked teenaged concert star, he had been her closest friend. He had been her first and only love. She had given up her father and battled in court to win the legal right to marry him. She had performed his music in concerts all over Europe. She had born him seven children and was now pregnant with the eighth. For thirteen years of marriage, she had stood by him, happy or unhappy, sick or well, rich or poor. Now, how would it all end?

"Him, the magnificent Robert, in an institution!" Clara wrote in her diary. It was an unbearable thought, her greatest sorrow.

Clara was only thirty-four years old, but she felt spent like an old woman. How could she go on caring for the children all by her herself? Who would provide for them? And who could possibly fill the emptiness in her heart that Robert had left?

Clara was desperate for help. She needed a friend, a best friend.

Chapter 14
Best Friends

The day before Robert left for Endenich, Johannes Brahms arrived in Düsseldorf. He announced to Clara the he had come to cheer her up with music, if that were her wish. He said he would do whatever he could to assist her. He promised, when Robert returned from the asylum, that he would visit with him until he regained his health.

Brahms took over the Schumanns' household accounts. He recorded all the money spent on servants' wages, rent, postage stamps, and other expenses, and noted royalties sent from Robert's music publisher.

Brahms rented a room in the same house in which the Schumanns lived. He earned a small amount of money teaching a few piano students, and he composed a little. He spent the rest of his time helping Clara maintain her household. He looked after the children's education and gave them music lessons.

The youngest Schumann child was born June 11, 1854. He was named Felix, after the composer and the Schumanns' friend, Felix Mendelssohn.

The large Schumann family needed money. Many musicians offered to play concerts to benefit them, but Clara wouldn't allow it. She said if concerts needed to be played for her family, she would play them herself. She was too proud to accept charity, and she needed to work. Practicing the piano and making concert arrangements kept her mind off Robert. While she was away on concert tours, Brahms stayed home and babysat the children.

The months dragged on. There seemed to be no change in Robert's health. Brahms' mother became upset. She sent angry letters to her son, urging him to get back to his own musical career. She told him that other people were willing to help the Schumanns and that servants could take care of their children. Brahms wouldn't listen to her. In a generous act of friendship, he sacrificed two years of his life to help out Robert and Clara.

Having Brahms around was a great consolation for Clara. He was very sensitive and understood why she loved Robert so much. Clara talked and talked about Robert, often bursting into tears. She was able to say things about him to Brahms that she couldn't say to anyone else. Clara also greatly admired Brahms. She knew he was a musical genius, just like she had known Robert was one, long before the rest of the world realized it. Clara shared music with Brahms in much the same way as she had shared it with Robert.

At first, Clara thought of Brahms like a son. Eventually, they developed deep, strong feelings for each other. Brahms and Clara fell in love. Many people have wondered what went on between them in private, but no one knows for sure. They never spoke to others about their relationship. Later, they burned their letters to each other. Clara was a very proper woman. Both she and Brahms were devoted to Robert. For these reasons, it is believed that Clara and Brahms did not become lovers.

Clara worried constantly about Robert. For a long time, she didn't know if he would ever get better. The doctors sent her a weekly report, but they didn't allow her to visit him. They felt the sight of Clara would upset him too much. Clara obeyed the doctors, believing that they knew best.

In Endenich, the grounds of the asylum were like a park, with trees, grass, and flower gardens. Robert had his own suite of comfortable rooms, furnished with a piano. He played the piano and composed a little. He slept many hours, probably because he was given heavy doses of tranquilizers. Robert was allowed to take long walks with his male nurse into nearby Bonn and the surrounding mountains. Some days he was calm, almost normal. He began to write letters to Clara. Brahms, Joachim, and other friends visited him.

After Robert had been in Endenich for two years, his mental health grew worse. The doctors told Clara that he would never recover his sanity.

Clara was on a concert tour of England when she received a telegram stating that Robert was close to death. He had refused to eat anything for a long time and was starving himself to death.

Clara and Brahms traveled to Endenich and visited Robert. Clara was shocked to see how thin he had become. He was too weak to talk, but he seemed happy to see her. She fed him a little beef gelatin and wine. Three days later, on July 29, 1856, while Clara and Brahms went to meet Joachim at the railway station, Robert died quietly and alone.

Clara was heart-broken, but she also felt relief. Robert no longer had to suffer. She wrote in her diary, "I stood at the body of my dearly loved husband and was calm; all my feelings were of the thankfulness to God that he was finally free."

Soon after Robert's death, Clara, her sons Ludwig and Ferdinand, Brahms, and his sister Elise took a month-long vacation together in Switzerland. At this time, Clara and Brahms might have discussed their future together.

There were many reasons why Clara wouldn't have wanted to remarry. Clara, fourteen years older than Brahms, probably thought she was too old for him. Also, married life meant having babies, and she already had enough children. Brahms was just starting his composing career and composers didn't usually make much money. Clara was devoted to the memory of Robert and wanted to continue on with the Schumann name. Probably most important of all, Clara wanted her independence. Being a wife in the nineteenth century meant helping a husband with his work, and Clara wanted to do her own work. Her marriage to Robert had often kept her from performing. Now she was eager to continue her concert career without having a duty toward any man.

After their vacation together, Clara and Brahms went their separate ways. Throughout their lives, they kept in touch through letters and visits. They still loved each other, but without the strong emotion they had once felt. They called themselves "best friends."

Clara told Brahms she hoped he would get married, and yet, whenever he got close to a younger woman, she became unhappy. Brahms once wrote to Joachim, "I think I can no longer love an unmarried girl . . . They but promise heaven while Clara shows it revealed to us."

Clara was a widow for forty years. Brahms remained a bachelor. They spent their lives apart, yet, in spirit, they were together. Brahms would live only eleven months longer than Clara.

Chapter 15
Widowhood

After Robert's death, Clara spent most of her time playing concerts, trying to earn a living. She was forced to split up her family in order to care for her children's needs. Marie, Elise, Ludwig, and Ferdinand went to boarding schools. Julie, who was thin and sickly, went to live with her grandmother Marianne in Berlin. The two small children, Eugenie and Felix, stayed home with housekeepers.

Clara traveled and performed ten months of the year. She didn't see her children very much. She could only be with them on vacations and sometimes at Christmas. She kept up with them by writing numerous letters. She also wrote to their teachers and the people who were taking care of them. The children missed their mother. Often, she was not there when they needed her most.

Brahms urged Clara not to work so much and to take time to be with the children. She told him she had to work hard to keep from getting depressed. She often looked sad. Only making music made her truly happy. Once when she was upset she wrote, "My true old friend, my piano, must help me with this!"

Clara worried about her children. Many of them had unhappy lives. Julie wanted to marry an Italian count. Clara thought that the man was too different from Julie and wouldn't make a good husband for her; however, she remembered how miserable she had been when her father wouldn't let her marry Robert. She gave Julie permission to marry the count. Julie had two children. She died of tuberculosis when she was twenty-seven.

Ludwig began to behave oddly around age thirteen. Clara sent him to trade school, but he couldn't learn a trade. At twenty, he wanted to become a pianist and composer. Clara tried to help him by giving him lessons, even though she didn't have any faith that he would succeed. A doctor told Clara that Ludwig had a disease of the spine that damaged his brain. At age twenty-two, Ludwig was committed to a mental institution. This caused Clara great misery, reminding her of Robert's insanity. Clara couldn't afford to send Ludwig to a private asylum. He had to go to a state institution that looked more like a prison. Clara visited Ludwig only a few times because it made her too sad to see him, and he always begged her to take him home. Ludwig lived twenty-nine years in the mental institution, until his death.

Ferdinand was drafted to fight in the Franco-Prussian War. He didn't get wounded, but suffered from rheumatism. The doctors gave him morphine for his pain, and he became addicted to it. He spent the rest of his life in and out of hospitals trying to cure his morphine habit. He died of addiction at age forty-two, leaving a widow and six children for Clara to support. Ferdinand's oldest son, also named Ferdinand, became a fine pianist.

Felix, the only Schumann child who never saw his father, looked the most like Robert and inherited his talent for writing. He wrote and published poetry. Brahms used some of Felix's poems as words for his songs. Unfortunately, Felix didn't have much time to develop his talent. He died of tuberculosis at twenty-four.

The Schumann girls, Marie, Elise, and Eugenie all became piano teachers. Marie never married, but stayed with Clara and worked as her assistant. Elise left home at age twenty and earned her living as a music teacher and a companion to wealthy women. At age thirty-four, she married a businessman and had four children. Like Marie, Eugenie never married. She taught with her mother and Marie for twenty years. At age forty, she moved to England to teach and perform. Eugenie wrote two books: *Memoirs* about her life in the Schumann family and *Robert Schumann: A Portrait of My Father.*

After Robert's death, Clara stopped composing. She had a talent for it, but she lacked confidence. Nineteenth century society told her it was impossible for women to compose great works. She wrote in her diary: "I once thought that I possessed creative talent, but I have given up this idea; a woman must not desire to compose. Not one has been able to do it, and why should I expect to? It would be arrogance." It took a long time for people to realize that women could compose as well as men. Today, there are many fine women composers.

Clara once enjoyed her composing, and she produced many fine works. Earlier she wrote: "There is no greater joy than composing something oneself and then listening to it." But composing was hard work for her, and piano playing came naturally. She thought her most important role was as a pianist interpreting Robert's music. She also edited his music for his publishers.

Toward the end of her life, Clara began to slow down. She suffered from rheumatism and arthritis. She also began to lose her hearing. At age fifty-nine she traveled less and played fewer concerts. She took a teaching position at the Hoch Conservatory of Music in Frankfurt.

In October 1878, Clara celebrated her silver jubilee as a concert pianist. It had been fifty years since she first walked onto the Gewandhaus stage as a young girl of nine. Clara's friends at Hoch Conservatory surprised her by playing a concert of her compositions. Another celebration took place in the Leipzig Gewandhaus. Clara performed Robert's piano concerto in a concert that featured his music. When she walked on stage the whole audience stood. Clara's fans threw flowers until her feet were buried. It took a long time for the audience to quiet down. Then Clara took her seat at the piano and played as she had done so many times before in the last fifty years.

Ten years later, Clara was honored on her sixtieth jubilee by even more concerts. Telegrams, flowers, wreaths, and poetry flooded in to her from all over the world. In 1891, at the age of seventy-two, Clara played her last public concert in Frankfurt. She continued to teach until she suffered a stroke in March 1896.

She never recovered. Two months later, as Clara lay dying, her grandson Ferdinand played for her some of Robert's music on the piano. She died quietly on May 20, 1896 at the age of seventy-six.

Clara Wieck Schumann had the longest concert career of any woman in the nineteenth century. She was named Royal and Imperial Virtuosa and created a new style of piano playing, instilling deep feeling into all the music she performed. She was the wife of Robert Schumann, the mother of eight children, and the "best friend' of Johannes Brahms. She worked as a piano teacher and editor of her husband's music. As a composer, she wrote some fine works, including piano pieces, songs, and *Piano Trio in G Minor.*

Clara Schumann worked hard all her life and achieved many accomplishments. Above all, this remarkable woman loved to play the piano for others. She wrote, "Art is a beautiful gift. What, indeed, is more beautiful than to clothe one's feeling in sound? What a comfort in sad hours, what a pleasure, what a wonderful feeling, to provide an hour of happiness to others."

Janet Nichols Lynch is the author of thirteen books including *American Music Makers: An Introduction to American Composers, Women Music Makers: An Introduction to Women Composers, Racing California,* a Society of School Librarians International Honor Book, and *Messed Up,* an ALA Quick-Pick for Reluctant Readers and a VOYA (Voices of Youth Advocates) Top of the Top Shelf Fiction for Middle School Readers. Her work has appeared in *The New Yorker, Seventeen,* and *Highlights for Children.*

Janet was born and raised in Sacramento. She graduated with a BA in Music from California State University, Sacramento; an MM in Piano from Arizona State; and an MFA in Creative Writing from California State University, Fresno. She has taught music, English, and history at the middle school, high school, and college levels. She lives with her husband in Visalia, California, and they have two grown children. She enjoys competing in runs and triathlons, and has the goal of cycling in every state. Find her at JanetNicholsLynch.com, Facebook.com/jnicholslynch, and Twitter @JanetNicLynch.

www.ingramcontent.com/pod-product-compliance
Lightning Source LLC
Chambersburg PA
CBHW031526040426
42445CB00009B/423